Sending Love...
My "Different-Functional" Family
By Lori Hilliard

Library of Congress Control Number: 2007943055
ISBN 13: 978-0-9801737-2-7
ISBN 10: 0-9801737-2-8
1st printing March 2009

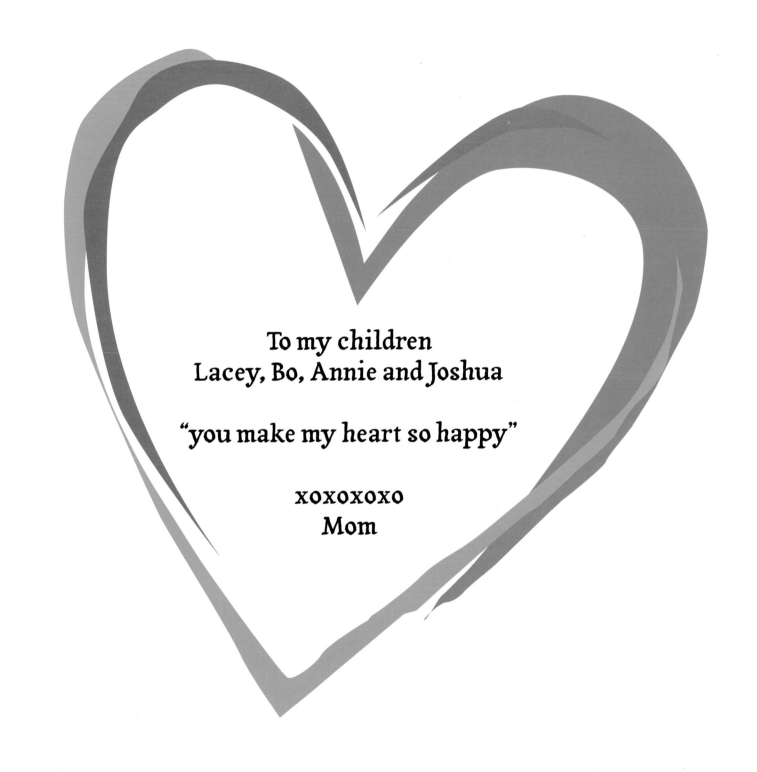

To my children
Lacey, Bo, Annie and Joshua

"you make my heart so happy"

xoxoxoxo
Mom

A note to the parents,

This story is told through the eyes of my five year old son, Joshua. When I went through my divorce, I looked and looked for a storybook I could share with him that would explain what was happening in his life and the lives of his siblings. I found several wonderful books published on the subject of divorce, but they mostly featured make-believe characters like talking teddy bears. I wanted a real child's face for Joshua to see and identify with that would help him to understand that other real children had been through a divorce and that it was not just a made up "character" story.

This book came about to fulfill that need. What I found was that I could not really address "DIVORCE" as a subject. That would take volumes to try to describe. What I could do was address what is left behind after divorce. Children identify so much with their parents, family, school and friends. When something happens and these are changed or altered, the child is left asking,

"WHO AM I?"

This book is written from my heart. Just like you, I want my children to understand that a divorce is not their fault. Just like you, I want them to know that they are LOVE, they were created in LOVE, and that they are still LOVED.....like crazy.

Every time I read this book to my children, they snuggle close to me and soak the love in. I wish this for your children as well. The back of this book has a special section for you to write your family's story. It provides the opportunity to include photographs and write your own personal commitment to your children.

In writing this book, I grew. I knew that I had to settle differences with my "ex" and, in the process, release my children from seeing our pain. One day in the early stages of putting this book together, I ran across a quote from Mister Rogers.

"So in all you do in all of your life, I wish you strength and the grace to make the choices which will allow you and your neighbor to become the best of whoever you are".

The miracle I experienced by writing this book was the healing of my own heart as I tried to live "strength" and "grace". It surprises me how true it is that when we give something away we only receive it back. My relationship with my children's father was completely transformed. He helped with the photography in this book. We teach our children that they are still part of a wonderful family.

As you turn the next few pages of this book, you will be introduced to Joshua's family.........a beautiful **"DIFFERENT-FUNCTIONAL"** family!

Lori Hilliard

joshua

My name is Joshua.

I am 5 years old.

I like to play in the dirt.

L brothers an

I have two sisters,
Lacey and Annie,

and one brother,
named Bo.

s·sters

B

I also have a cat
and a dog,

and two birds named Jack and Jill... and they had a baby I named "Hill".

I live by
the mountains,

and I live by
the lake.

I have two houses.

I have a great time being
ME!

At my
Dad's house
I love to
swim and
catch fish.

At my Mom's house I love to catch lizards and play at the park!

My parents are "Divorced".

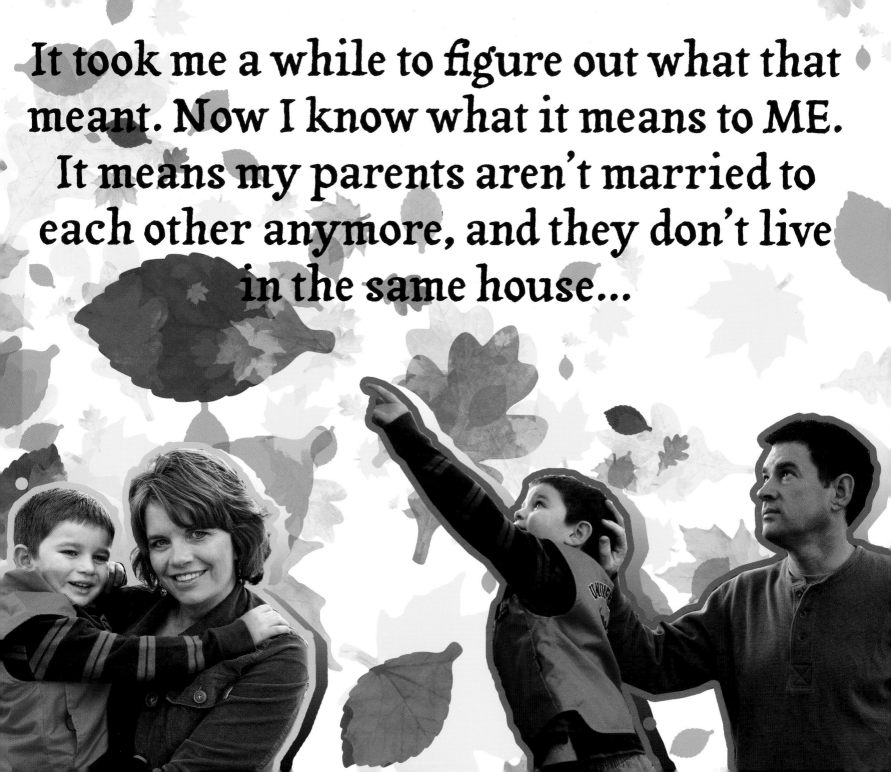

It took me a while to figure out what that meant. Now I know what it means to ME. It means my parents aren't married to each other anymore, and they don't live in the same house...

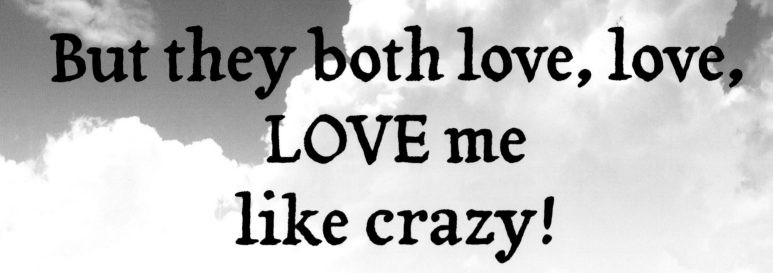

But they both love, love, LOVE me like crazy!

(And with all of their hearts!!!!!!!)

I live with my Mom and my sister Annie, and we go to school where my Mom lives.

My brother Bo and my sister Lacey live with my Dad, and they go to school where my Dad lives.

My brother and sisters LOVE my Dad SO MUCH!!! He always makes us laugh.

We all LOVE my Mom, too! I sometimes say to her, "Mom, I love you to the moon, the stars, and the sky THIRTY-MILLION times," because I know that is A LOT!!!

One day someone asked my Mom, "Is your family DYSFUNCTIONAL?" (That is a big "grown-up" word.)

I like to learn about words...and that word means that something is WRONG.

My Mom just smiled when she answered and said we are not Dysfunctional... We are only

"Different" -Functional

Sometimes people have things in their life that are not the SAME as everyone else. But that does not make them wrong...it just means they are different.

And most of the time, the things that make us different can also make us that much more SPECIAL!

I know that I am SPECIAL because I have
so many people to love...

and so many people who love

me.

Now it's your turn to tell your story.

This is Me!

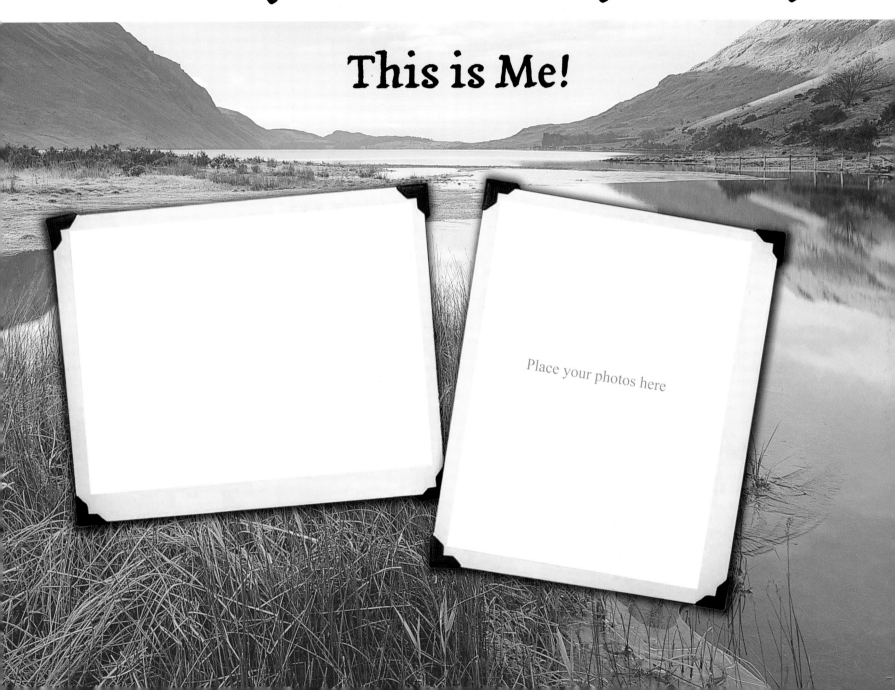

Place your photos here

THIS IS MY MOM.

THIS IS MY DAD.

THIS IS OUR FAMILY.

HERE ARE SOME THINGS I LIKE TO DO.

SPECIAL TIMES

MY MOM AND DAD LOVE ME VERY MUCH.
THIS IS WHAT MY MOM AND DAD THINK
ABOUT WHEN THEY THINK ABOUT ME.

_____
_____
_____
_____
_____
_____
_____
_____
_____
_____
_____

_____   _____
Dad's Signature   Mom's Signature